LIGHTING

AND ACCESSORIES
17th – 19th CENTURIES

by Stan Hamper

History — Illustrations — Descriptions

About the Author

Stan Hamper enjoyed a life filled with many interests. As a young boy in the scouting program he earned the rank of Eagle Scout with silver palm and as an adult was the recipient of the Silver Beaver. A veteran of the Navy during WWII, he saw service in the Atlantic, Mediterranean, and Pacific theaters. After service he trained as an archaeologist and had three year's experience in the Southwest. More recently he was active in research and development engineering and served as chief engineer in several corporations. His hobbies included watercolor portraiture, pen and ink, wood carving, and model design and building, as well as collecting early American lighting.

He was founding director of the Southwestern Michigan College Museum 1981 — 1992. After retiring he continued his interest in research and writing. He served as volunteer curator for the National Heddon Museum from 1995 until his death on October 22, 1998.

Hamper's first book, *Wilderness Survival,* written in 1963, was sold nationally and used as a textbook by the National Camping Association and the Colorado Outward Bound School. The book was also widely used by scout groups, canoe outfitters, and by those walking the Appalachian Trail.

Historical Reflections of Cass County, compiled for the Cass County Historical Commission in 1981, was Hamper's first book on area history. It was primarily a reference for recognizing architecturally and historically significant homes in Cass County, Michigan.

A third book, *Waterpowered Mills in Cass County,* published in 1993, pointed out the significance of water power in that area's development. Volumes I and II of *Dowagiac Stories — Windows to the Past* were published in 1996 and 1998. These two books bring to light stories which prove this Southwestern Michigan community is indeed an historic treasure.

This volume is being published posthumously through the efforts of his widow, Margaret L. Hamper, who gave support, advice, and encouragement on earlier books. Hamper acknowledged her help with a handwritten inscription: To Margaret: For dotting the i's, crossing the t's with patience and love! (written in her personal copy of Volume I of *Dowagiac Stories*).

Cover design: Beth Summers
Book design: Holly C. Long
Illustrations: Stan Hamper

Collector Books

P.O. Box 3009

Paducah, KY 42002-3009

www.collectorbooks.com

Copyright © 2002 by Margaret Hamper

Contents

Introduction

No attempt has been made in this work to include illustrations of all types of lighting devices and related items found in America into the early part of the twentieth century.

Many hundreds of examples of types originating from basic designs were created. Since many were made by the local blacksmith, tinsmith, or handyman, a basic type will show subtle or obvious variation in design and workmanship resulting in various degrees of quality.

With these qualifications in mind, the reader will note that the illustrations are for the most part composites, giving dimensional ranges rather than specific sizes. A few examples, which are in the writer's collection or which have been examined and which appear to be more or less standard, list specific dimensions.

The collector examining specific pieces should expect to find dimensional variations as well as differences in design and quality.

Each year diminishes the number of lighting devices available to the collector, and of course prices are increasing dramatically in many instances. As a result, it becomes necessary when compiling a collector's guide to keep the average collector in mind and to concentrate on those lighting devices available at reasonable prices.

General price variations become obvious as one travels in different areas of the country. There may also be considerable variation in prices between dealers in the same area. For example, I noted a miner's hat lamp in one shop priced at $29.50. The identical lamp in comparable condition was priced at $195.00 in a shop less than 20 miles away. The realistic price was somewhere in between.

Condition is certainly an important criteria in establishing value. The amount of restoration, either obvious or otherwise, should be considered. In the writer's opinion, an unaltered device with a few dents, a cracked or missing glass, or some rust has far greater value than a device indicating wood or metal parts replacement, signs of new solder, new nails, replaced glass, rivets, and so forth.

Restoration, unless undertaken by experts after careful study, may destroy much of the value of a piece since the parts replaced may not truly represent the size, shape, or design intent of the original maker.

The collector should feel free to ask the seller for information concerning the piece being considered for purchase. The seller should be willing to supply all facts at his disposal regarding age, authenticity, etc.

In closing, remember: buyer beware. Build your collection carefully. There are still many good lighting devices available. You must be the final judge in determining age, authenticity, availability, and the price you are willing to pay.

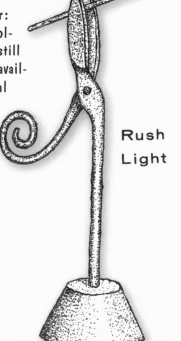

Rush
Light

Lighting Devices
A Brief History

The history of lighting began many centuries ago when primitive man learned to control and, hence, to use fire. He adopted it as a source for warmth, for cooking, and for light.

No one can be certain whether he learned to make fire by friction or by creating sparks. However, once he had mastered a method, fire became a part of life, and the light it created became an important and natural adjunct.

Since the earliest known lighting devices were rocks with shallow depressions which held burnable fats and oils and a simple moss or fiber wick, it seems logical to speculate that such simple devices resulted from observations made while fatty meat was being cooked.

A piece of meat held over fire melted the fats which in turn dripped into the fire causing momentary spurts of bright light. A piece of unwanted fat thrown into the fire would also cause a brighter flame. Why not place some fat in a container, introduce a flame to burn it, and produce a light?

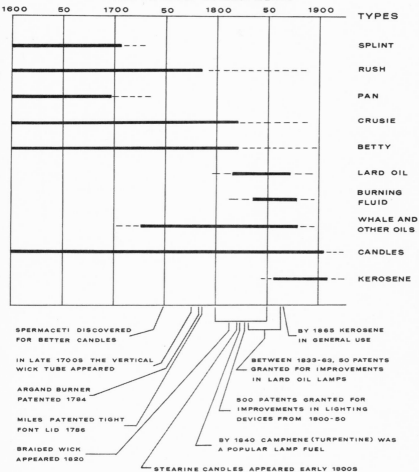

LIGHTING DEVICES - THEIR PERIODS OF USE
AND PRIMARY DEVELOPMENTS

TYPES

SPLINT

RUSH

PAN

CRUSIE

BETTY

LARD OIL

BURNING FLUID

WHALE AND OTHER OILS

CANDLES

KEROSENE

SPERMACETI DISCOVERED FOR BETTER CANDLES

IN LATE 1700S THE VERTICAL WICK TUBE APPEARED

ARGAND BURNER PATENTED 1784

MILES PATENTED TIGHT FONT LID 1786

BRAIDED WICK APPEARED 1820

BY 1865 KEROSENE IN GENERAL USE

BETWEEN 1833-63, 50 PATENTS GRANTED FOR IMPROVEMENTS IN LARD OIL LAMPS

500 PATENTS GRANTED FOR IMPROVEMENTS IN LIGHTING DEVICES FROM 1800-50

BY 1840 CAMPHENE (TURPENTINE) WAS A POPULAR LAMP FUEL

STEARINE CANDLES APPEARED EARLY 1800S

First Lamps

Obviously such discovery and use have been oversimplified here since learning to make even the first crude lamp probably required a long period of trial and error. Nevertheless, once the first successful primitive lamp was created, the history of light was underway. There was very little change in the basic concept of lighting for many centuries. Oils and greases continued to be the sources of fuel, although the types of vessels used to hold the fuel did show a conscious effort to improve.

Earliest vessels were of stone with natural depressions. Later varieties were of worked stone. After the discovery and development of ceramics, a great variety of lamps was made. Some were of simple design for a single wick, while others were quite grand with many wicks being used. The use of metals allowed for an even greater variety of lighting devices although better fuels continued to be the limiting factor in development.

Rush and Splint Lights

Judging by man's continuing struggle for a better life, it seems only natural that he experimented with other burnable materials with which he was familiar.

He certainly was aware of the heat and flame which could be extracted from a piece of resinous wood or a tough knot. At some time in prehistory he adapted the use of splints of resinous wood as a light source. When ignited, the splint would burn with varying degrees of speed and brightness, depending upon the resin content of the wood in relation to the angle above horizontal in which the splint was held. For example, a burning stick held horizontally will burn more rapidly than one held at a 45-degree angle.

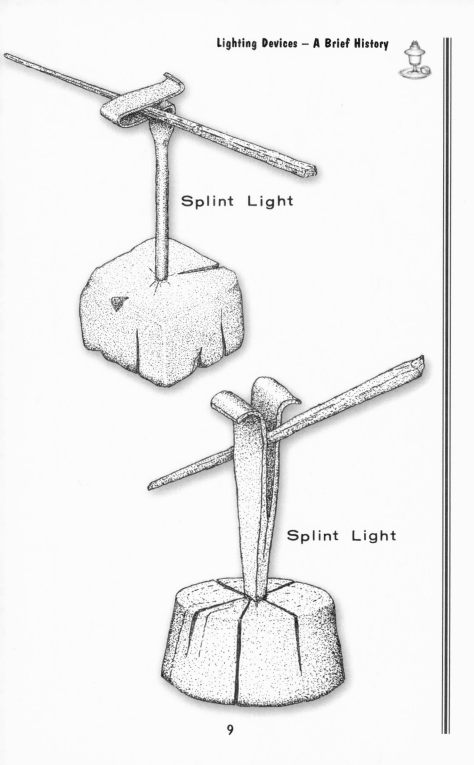

Splint Light

Splint Light

9

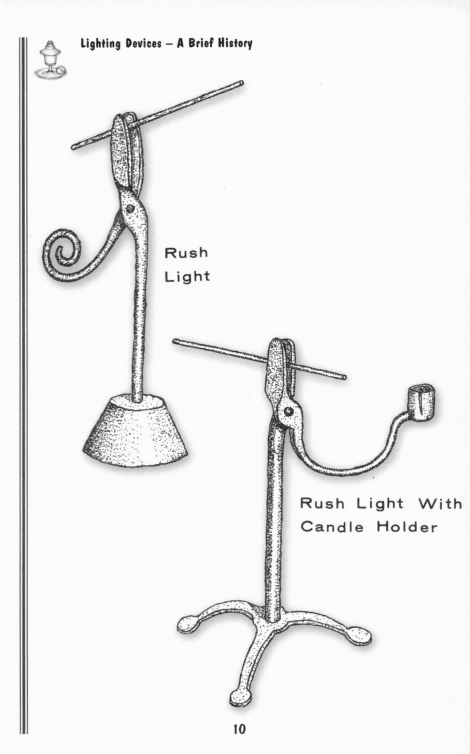

Rush
Light

Rush Light With
Candle Holder

Candles, Lamps, and Lanterns

The candle was another unique invention with its development spanning many centuries, starting probably during the first century A.D.

The candle wick is ignited, creating heat. This heat in turn melts then vaporizes the fuel surrounding the wick. The burning wick then burns the vapor to produce light.

Early tallow candles were far from satisfactory. They were smelly, smoky, and burned erratically. The twisted wick had a tendency to collect carbon and remain intact, seriously lowering the level of light. Constant light could be maintained only be removing the carbonized portion of the wick at frequent intervals. This process was called snuffing.

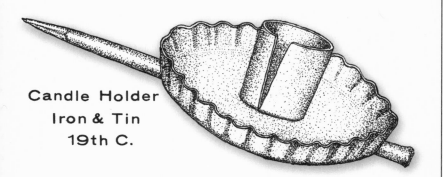

Candle Holder
Iron & Tin
19th C.

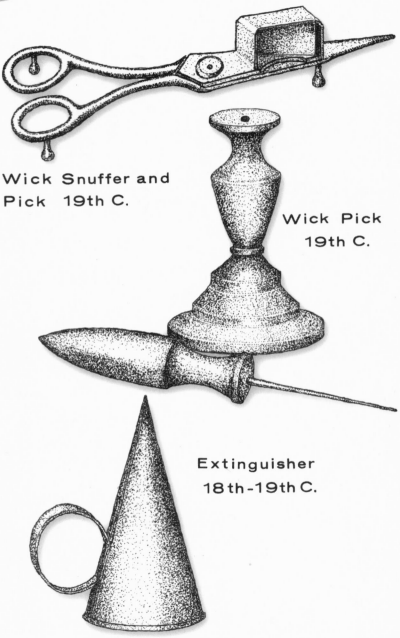

Wick Snuffer and
Pick   19th C.

Wick Pick
19th C.

Extinguisher
18th-19th C.

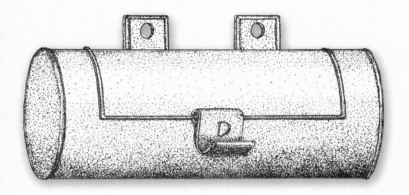

Tin Candle Box
19th C.

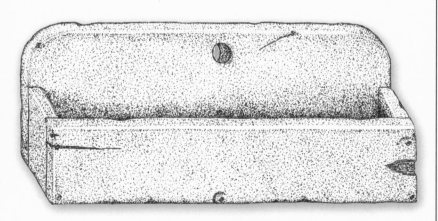

Wood Candle Box
18th C.

During the early part of the nineteenth century, processes were developed to extract stearine from tallow and other natural fats. Stearine had a higher melting point, was not greasy, and did not smoke or give off an unpleasant odor. Importantly it was not inclined to gutter – gutter meaning to eject rivulets of molten fuel.

Spermaceti, beeswax, bayberry wax, and paraffin had also been used in candle manufacture.

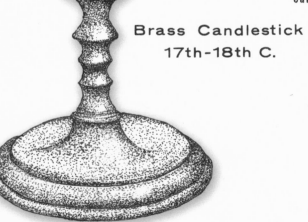

At about the same time that stearine was developing as a candle fuel, the braided wick replaced the earlier twisted variety and eliminated the need for snuffing almost entirely.

Candles continue to be efficient light producers, although their primary purpose has changed from utilitarian to a more casual one. Their use over many hundreds of years instigated the design and construction of literally thousands of one-of-a-kind candle holders as well as the continuing production of a vast variety of manufactured types.

**Brass Candlestick
17th-18th C.**

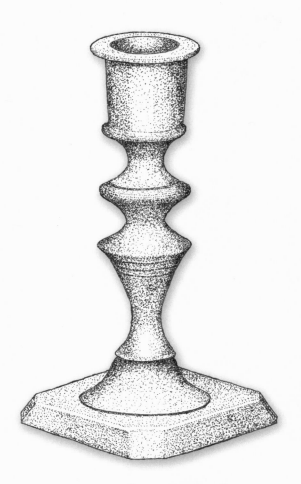

Brass "Bee Hive"
Candlestick
19th C.

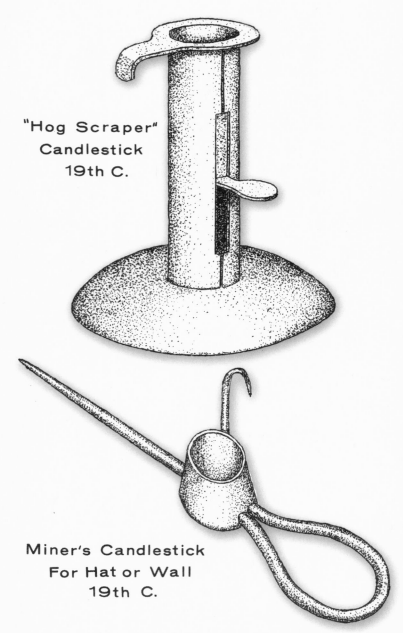

"Hog Scraper"
Candlestick
19th C.

Miner's Candlestick
For Hat or Wall
19th C.

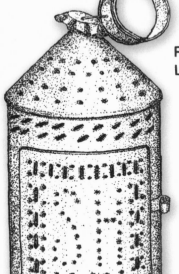

Pierced Tin Candle
Lantern 18th-19th C.

Spiral Candlestick
18th C.

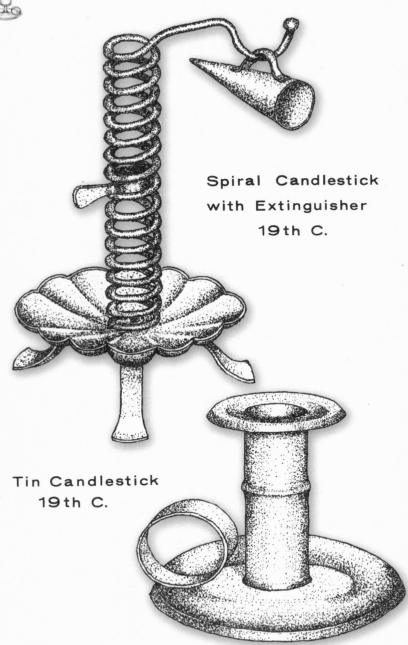

Spiral Candlestick
with Extinguisher
19th C.

Tin Candlestick
19th C.

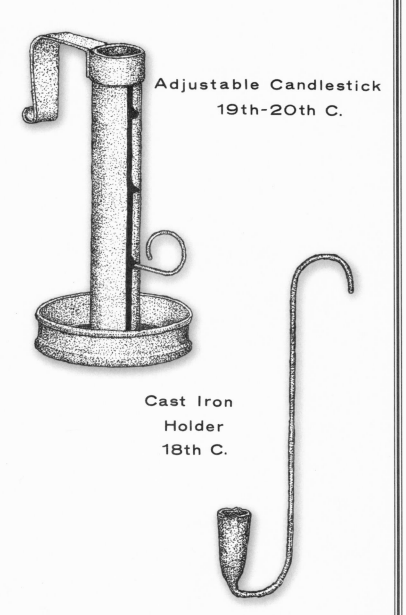

Adjustable Candlestick
19th-20th C.

Cast Iron
Holder
18th C.

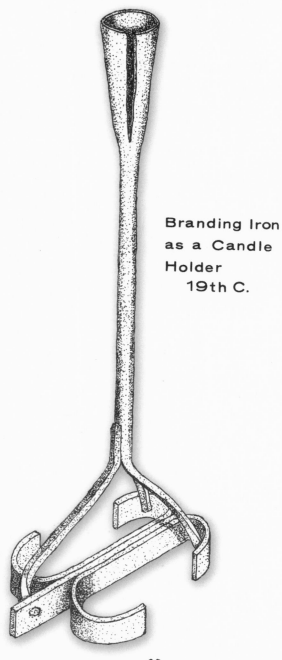

Branding Iron
as a Candle
Holder
19th C.

20

Iron Candle Holder
Civil War Period
19th C.

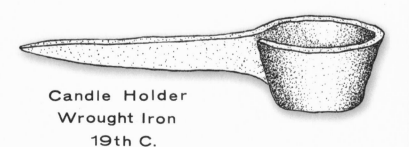

Candle Holder
Wrought Iron
19th C.

RR. Coach Lamp
19th C.

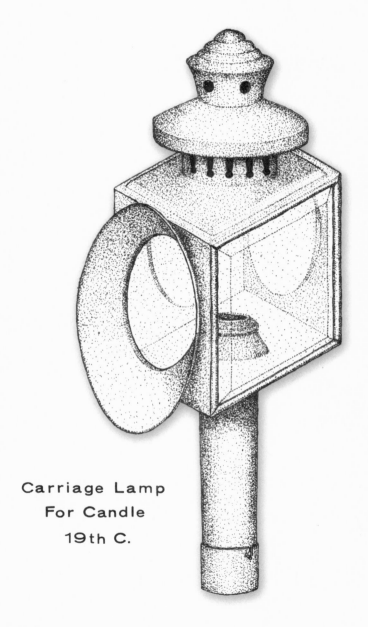

Carriage Lamp
For Candle
19th C.

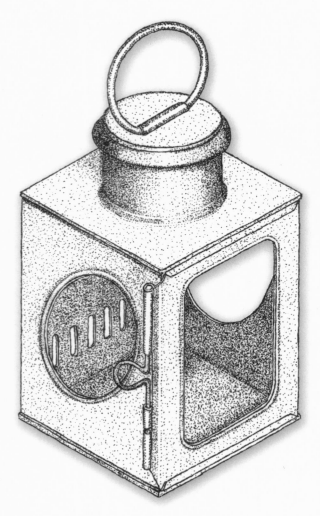

Candle Lantern
19th C.

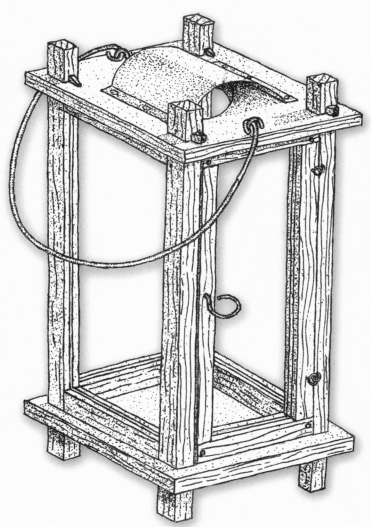

Wood Lantern
19th C.

Wood Lantern
19th C.

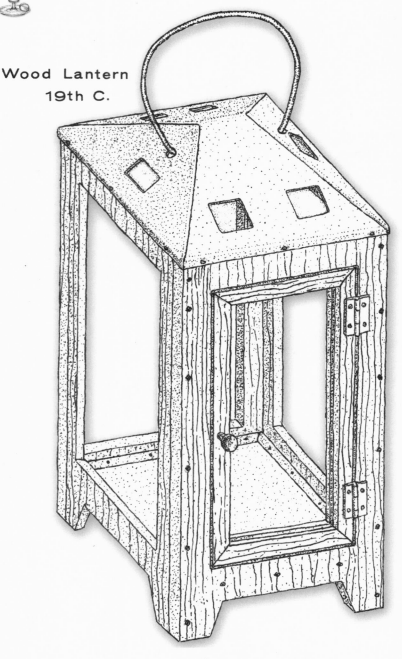

Tin Sconce
19th C.

Tin Sconce
19th C.

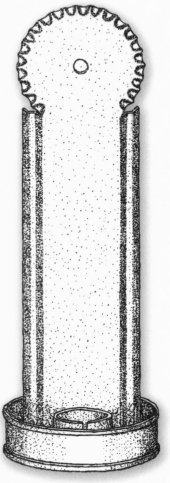

Tin Sconce
19th C.

Tin Sconce
19th C.

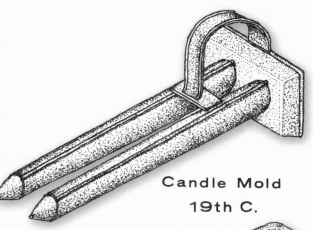

Candle Mold
19th C.

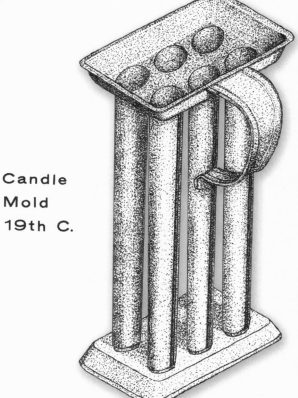

Candle
Mold
19th C.

Grease and Oil Lamp Types

Grease and oil lamps originated in Europe and arrived in America with the earliest settlers. Their manufacture and use continued into the mid-nineteenth century. Certainly some were still in use in remote and impoverished areas into the twentieth century since they afforded a source for light from fuel obtained from hunting, fishing, and butchering — the oil, tallow, and suet being saved and used.

This series of lighting devices gives one the opportunity to see firsthand the transition from the simple grease pan to the more sophisticated betty lamp and to follow this more or less logical development.

There are, in the opinion of many writers, three basic types of grease/oil lamps — the pan, crusie, and betty. However a collector may feel more at home with a broader listing of five, the pan, the pan with wick guide, the single crusie, the double crusie, and finally, the betty.

THE FIVE BASIC STAGES IN LAMP DEVELOPMENT FROM A SIMPLE PAN TO THE BETTY SHOWN IN SECTION AT A—A.

THERE WERE MANY DESIGN VARIATIONS.

NEW IDEAS DID NOT ALWAYS IMMEDIATELY REPLACE THE OLD.

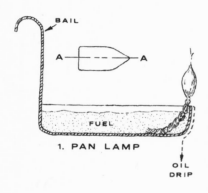

BAIL

A———————A

FUEL

1. PAN LAMP

OIL
DRIP

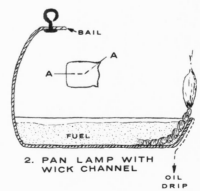

BAIL

A

A

FUEL

2. PAN LAMP WITH
WICK CHANNEL

OIL
DRIP

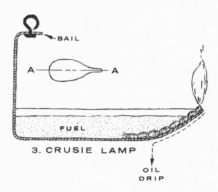

3. CRUSIE LAMP

OIL DRIP

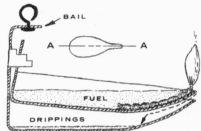

4. DOUBLE CRUSIE LAMP
(OR PHOEBE)

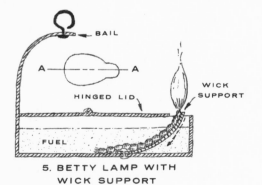

5. BETTY LAMP WITH
WICK SUPPORT

Pan, Crusie, and Betty Lamps

The pan lamp as the name implies is a simple shallow pan probably never more than five inches as the largest base dimension, and with sides seldom more than ½" high. The pan is usually equipped with a loop handle or one of a number of arm arrangements which allows the pan to be hung.

The pan was filled with fuel and a twisted wick inserted at any point against the rim to keep the wick end above the fuel. Such lamps were messy since excessive fuel had a tendency to drip from the wick onto any surface below.

I believe, as time passed, the makers of pan lamps added a wick holder to keep the wick in place during burning and to make it somewhat easier to extract the wick from the hardened fuel after a period of non-use. The holder was a simple, then, angular trough extending out from the edge of the pan rim for about ½" and then tapering back to the side of the pan at its base.

The crusie with its long wick trough seems a natural next step in development. Although some have suggested the wick channel had little purpose beyond that function, I suggest that its size alone denotes greater purpose. It is my belief that the crusie's wick channel served first as a fuel preheater. Before lighting the wick, a hot coal could be held under the channel, melting or at least softening the fuel and giving the wick a somewhat easier time in vaporizing the fuel. Secondly, the wick, once lighted, would transmit some heat through the small wick channel, helping to keep the fuel soft around the wick.

Early crusies like the pan lamps were messy and dripped excess fuel. Later models eliminated the problem by adding a second pan of the same size and shape below the burner unit. Drippings could be caught, saved, and used again. Hence the double crusie — sometimes called a phoebe lamp.

Pan Lamps
18th C.

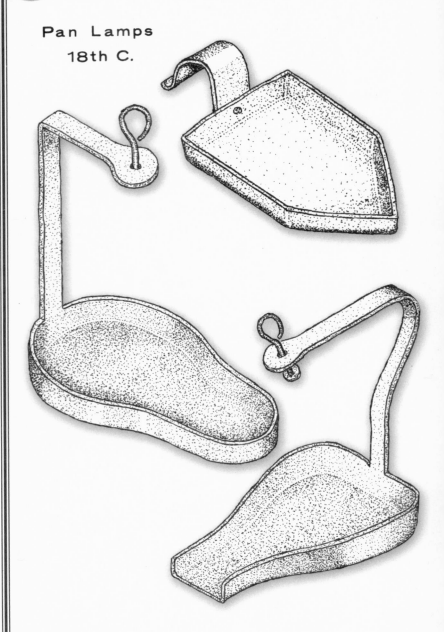

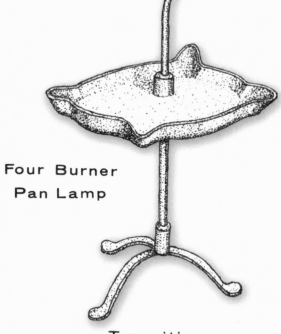

Four Burner
Pan Lamp

Transition
From Pan to Crusie

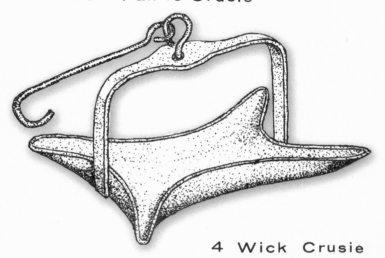

4 Wick Crusie

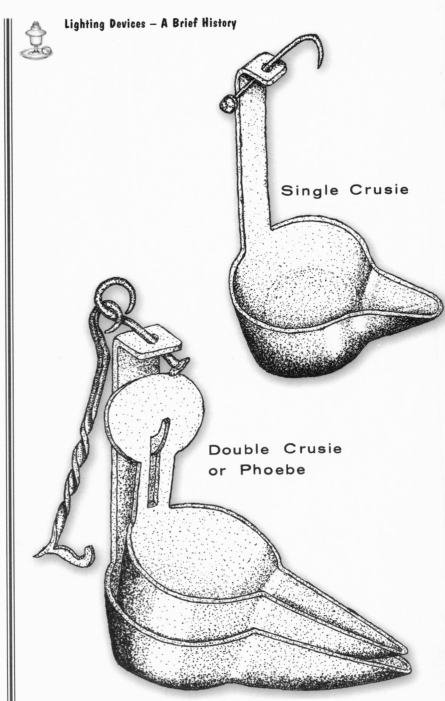

Single Crusie

Double Crusie
or Phoebe

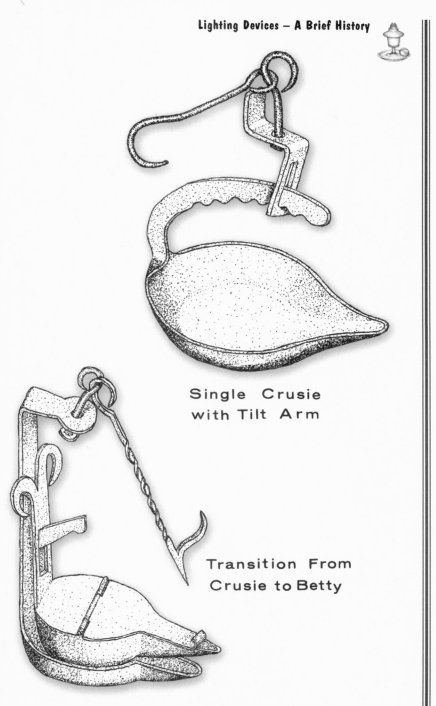

Single Crusie
with Tilt Arm

Transition From
Crusie to Betty

The transition from double crusie to the betty lamp seemed again to be a logical step forward. The betty lamp, usually pear shaped — a modification of the sharp nosed crusie, included a wick support within the body of the lamp, thus eliminating the dripping problem.

The betty also had a hinged or pivoted lid, probably aiding somewhat in warming the fuel, as well as eliminating the flying insect problem, at least to some degree.

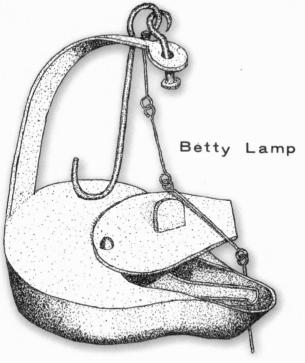

Betty Lamp

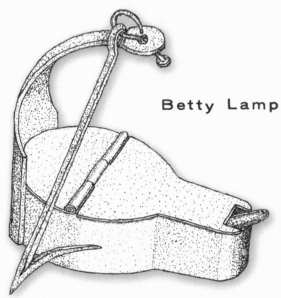

Betty Lamp

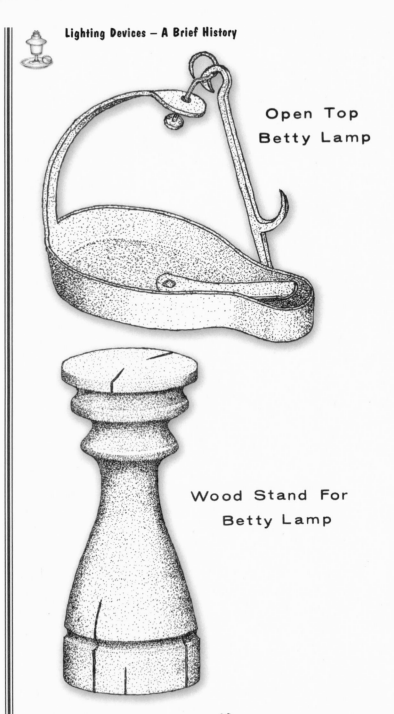

Open Top
Betty Lamp

Wood Stand For
Betty Lamp

Whale Oil Lamps

Between the late seventeenth and mid-eighteenth centuries, whale oil was in great demand as a fuel for lighting devices. Consumption at its peak of use was estimated at nearly a million gallons yearly.

Whale oil was easy to use, safe, and gave off little smoke. The odor was not too objectionable. Although it appears certain that whale oil was burned in crusies and bettys, it came into its own with the development of the vertical wick support in the late eighteenth century. Whale oil lamps required little attention beyond occasional wick adjustment. There were a great many varieties of whale oil lamps produced in tin, pewter, brass, silver, and glass, with less dense single or double wicks. The wicks were held vertically by wick support tubes extending about ½" above the font cap and for an inch or more into the font. There was also more often a slot in the side of the tube above the cap for wick adjustment.

Whale Oil Lamp
About 1840

Whale Oil "Petticoat"
Mid 1800s

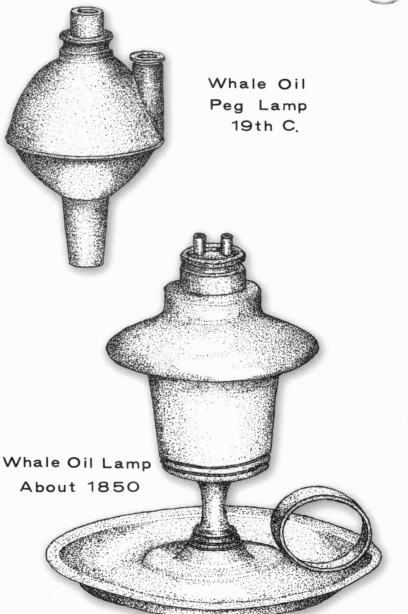

Whale Oil
Peg Lamp
19th C.

Whale Oil Lamp
About 1850

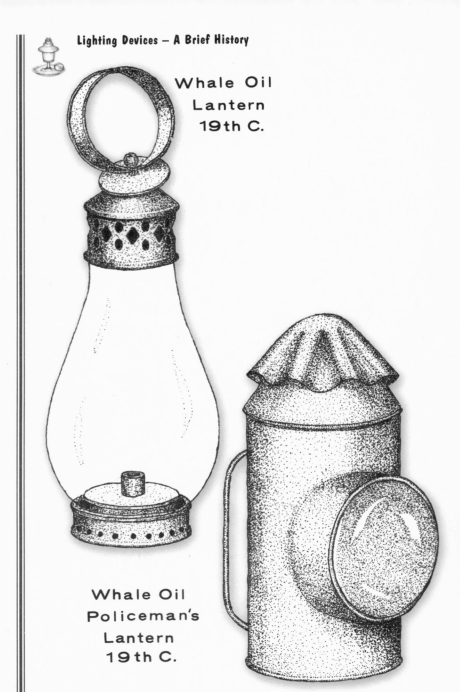

Whale Oil
Lantern
19th C.

Whale Oil
Policeman's
Lantern
19th C.

Burning Fluid Lamp
Glass Font
19th C.

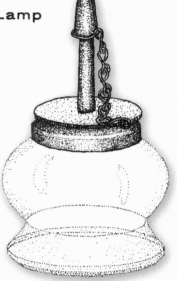

Burning Fluid
Petticoat Lamp
19th C.

45

CROSS SECTION VIEWS OF THE THREE TYPES OF VERTICAL WICK TUBE BURNERS.

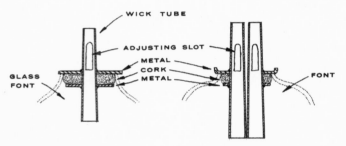

1. Single burner with metal and cork burner parts.

2. Double burner.

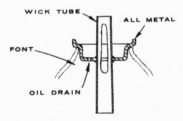

3. An all metal single burner.

DROP BURNERS, AS SHOWN ABOVE, CAME INTO COMMON USE ABOUT 1750, FIRST ON GLASS FONT LAMPS.

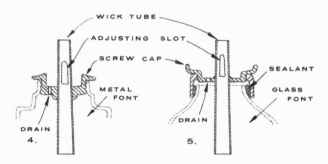

THE SCREW CAP FONT PATENTED BY
MILES IN 1784 AND FIRST USED WITH A
METAL FONT(4.) AND LATER ADAPTED
TO THE GLASS FONT(5.) REPLACING THE
DROP BURNER.

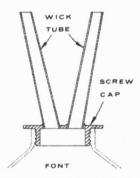

A TYPICAL BURNER FOR A
BURNING FLUID LAMP

Metal lamps used screw caps while early glass lamps had a drop burner — a cork lid through which the burner extended. Later glass varieties also had metal screw caps.

Although oils were recognized as having the greatest potential as lamp fuel, they were far too expensive for the average family, as well as being inaccessible in many areas. The vertical wick had also proved its superiority.

Since lard was the closest to fluid of the common fats, would burn well while in a fluid state, and was a common by-product of pork production, the challenge was to design a lighting device capable of melting lard.

Between 1800 and 1860 a number of attempts were made to solve the problem — some 50 patents were granted. Judging from available information, most methods devised met with only limited success — one could almost say a seasonal success.

Lard melted and poured into a lamp during warm weather stayed liquid almost indefinitely with the aid of room temperature and heat generated by the flame. However, when the air surrounding the lamp was cool, the lard quickly solidified.

Three burners seem to have shared what success there was: the ribbon burner, and the Argand and Southworth patent burners. The ribbon burner was the simplest solution. A long narrow wick support of copper was attached to the font cap. It extended above the cap for ½" or less and deep into the font. The copper conducted the heat from the burning wick down into the font where it either melted the lard and/or kept it in a fluid state.

Since the amount of light given off by a lighting device was also of primary concern, the Argand and Southworth patents used double wicks which increased the amount of light while at the same time intensified the amount of heat transmitted to the font to melt the lard and maintain it in a fluid state.

The Argand burner was designed to introduce additional oxygen for the twin flames. An air tube passed up through the font from the lamp base, through the font cap between the wick holders where it was most needed for better burning. The wick supports were of tin or copper, the copper being far better.

The Southworth patent was based on the heat transmission of copper. The wick supports were wide, flat copper pieces, like those in the Argand burner. Extensions of the width supports, also of copper, extended deep into the font in a loop, creating maximum heating surface.

As was mentioned earlier, there were a number of patents awarded for lard oil lamp improvements. However, these lamps were made in only limited quantity due to their lack of success. Finding one would indeed be rare.

In the mid-nineteenth century many attemps were made — often with disastrous results — to use highly volatile fuels for lamps. Camphene (turpentine) was the basic fuel ingredient with alcohol, benzine or naphtha added in various amounts.

Such fuel had a low flash point and required careful handling in special burners. Keeping the flame away from the fuel was the basic consideration and camphene lamps were designed accordingly.

Burning fluid lamps are easily identified by the length of the wick supports, usually over one inch long. Such supports were usually larger at their base than at the wick end, did not have wick adjusting slots, and did not extend down below the cap into the font. In examples with more than one wick, the tubes diverged from the cap at about a 15-degree angle to minimize the concentration of heat and to give each wick maximum oxygen for a brighter flame.

Most lamps of this type were supplied with caps suspended by small chains to place over the wick to minimize evaporation while not in use. However, the caps and chains are often missing although small holes in the font cap can be used as evidence that caps and chains were originally supplied.

The differences between whale oil and camphene burners are obvious, although since whale oil lamps were made and used prior to camphene and could easily be converted to camphene, such lamps have been occasionally mismarked as being whale oil and vice versa.

By 1860 a new age in lighting was underway. The continuing improvement in refining techniques and the resulting availability made kerosene the best and cheapest fuel. It was a good illuminant, clean burning if used properly, and was far safer than earlier volatile fuel.

The study of kerosene lighting devices is in itself a major undertaking, representing a nearly limitless variety of designs, patents, and applications.

DESIGN PRINCIPLES OF THE THREE BASIC
LARD OIL BURNER TYPES

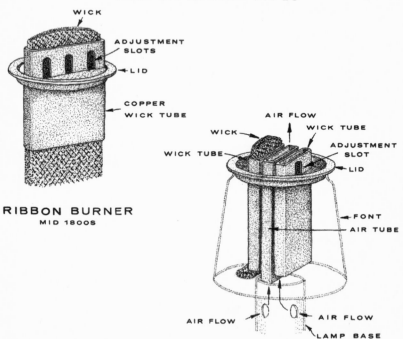

WICK

ADJUSTMENT
SLOTS

LID

COPPER
WICK TUBE

RIBBON BURNER
MID 1800S

AIR FLOW

WICK · WICK TUBE

WICK TUBE · ADJUSTMENT
SLOT

LID

FONT

AIR TUBE

AIR FLOW · AIR FLOW

LAMP BASE

ARGAND BURNER
PATENTED 1784

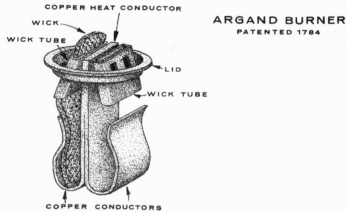

COPPER HEAT CONDUCTOR

WICK

WICK TUBE

LID

WICK TUBE

COPPER CONDUCTORS

SOUTHWORTH BURNER
PATENTED JULY 1842

Additional Examples of Early Lighting

Star Tumbler

Skater's Lamp
Kerosene
20th C.

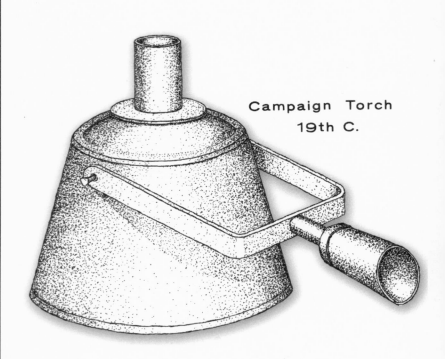

Campaign Torch
19th C.

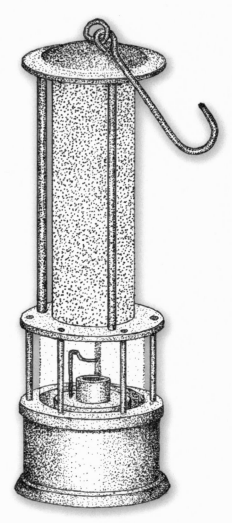

Miner's
Safety Lamp
19th-20th C.

Miner's Lamp
Cast Iron
19th C.

Miner's Lamp
Early 20th C.

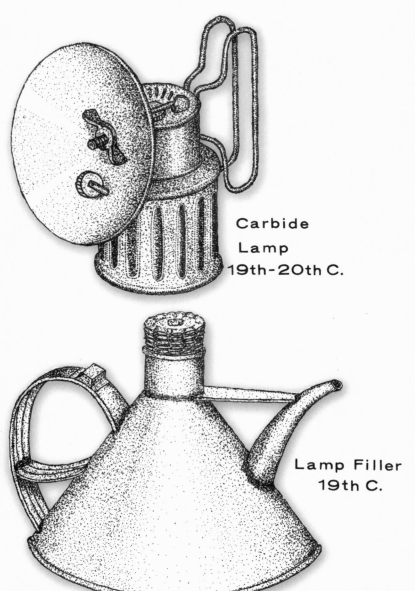

Carbide
Lamp
19th-20th C.

Lamp Filler
19th C.

Accessories

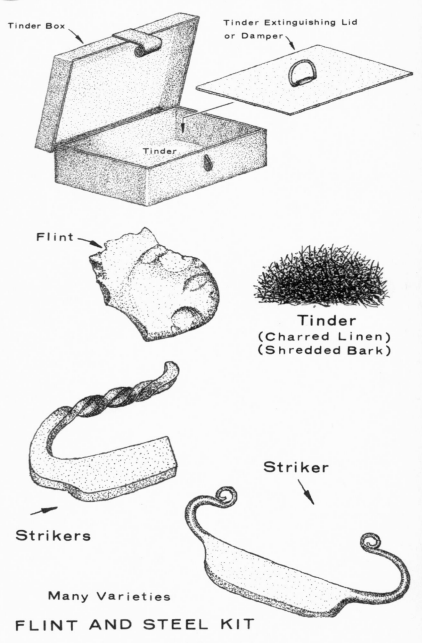

Tinder Box

Tinder Extinguishing Lid or Damper

Tinder

Flint

Tinder
(Charred Linen)
(Shredded Bark)

Strikers

Striker

Many Varieties

FLINT AND STEEL KIT

58

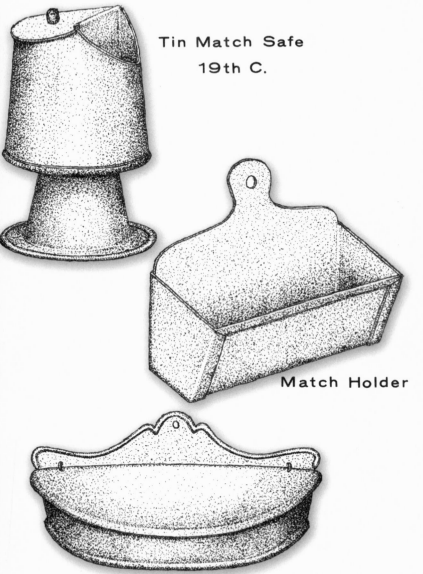

Tin Match Safe
19th C.

Match Holder

Tin Match Safe
19th-20th C.

Glossary of Terms

Terms, as applied to lighting devices, are often interchanged and may at times be misleading since authors may use terms which give various shades of meaning.

The glossary of terms which follows seems to be the most generally accepted definition and will hopefully be of help to the reader.

Alcohol — A colorless, volatile liquid which burns with a soft blue and yellow flame. Sometimes used by itself as lamp fuel but usually for small heaters. It was combined with turpentine in camphene lamps. Also see Camphene.

Argand burner — A burner patented in 1784, usually associated with lard oil lamps. Air to promote better burning was introduced through the lamp base, flowing up to the flames in a tube located between parallel wicks.

Bayberry wax (see Candle)

Benzine — A volatile liquid, a petroleum derivative sometimes mixed with turpentine to form a fuel for liquid fuel lamps. Also see Camphene.

Betty lamps — Early metal lamps of tin, iron, copper, and rarely, pewter. Most often were pear shaped but occasionally heart or oval. A wick support was located within the body of the lamp to eliminate dripping. They were seldom more than one inch deep and most had a hinged or swivel cover; most also included a half bail for hanging.

Burning fluid — In the context of this book, burning fluid was a mixture of turpentine (camphene) and alcohol, and sometimes benzine or naphtha.

Burning fluid lamps — Lamps with from one long vertical to six divergent round wick tubes. The tubes were usually smaller at the wick than at their base, had no wick adjusting slot, and did not extend down into the font.

Camphene — A term applied to turpentine. Somewhat misleading in referring to camphene lamps since such lamps burned a combination of camphene and alcohol or camphene and benzine or naphtha.

Campaign lantern — A lantern designed especially for campaigns and rallies. The glass panels were often decorated with campaign slogans. Some were illuminated with burning fuel lamps, but most by candles.

Campaign torch — One of a variety of metal torches used to illuminate night campaign marches and rallies. They were often suspended at the ends of long poles. Some were designed to be worn on hats, and others with a wood base were made to sit on a table or stage. Kerosene was usually used as fuel.

Candle — A solid fuel burner, a wick surrounded by fuel. Made originally of tallow with a twisted wick. Such candles were inefficient, smelly, messy, and the wick required constant attention to maintain a good level of illumination. Candles were later made of spermaceti, beeswax, bayberry wax, paraffin, and stearine. A braided wick eliminated the problem encountered with the twisted varieties.

Candle accessories — Include wick picks, snuffers, fire makers, save-alls (a container for holding short candle ends for remelting), storage containers of wood and metal, candle molds, extinguishers, etc.

Candle making — The process of placing wicks in molds, adding melted tallow, stearine, or wax, and allowing the candles to harden in the molds. Candles were also made by dipping wicks into melted fuel, removing the coated wick, and allowing the fuel to harden. This process was repeated until the candles reached the required diameter.

Candle molds — Tube shapes made of metal, glass, or ceramic. A wick was held in position down the center of the tube and melted fuel poured in around it. After the fuel had set up, the mold tubes were heated slightly and the finished candles were pulled out of the mold by the wick end.

Candle holders — One of the vast variety of devices both manufactured and homemade to hold a candle upright for burning. The group would include lanterns, candle sticks, wall sconces, chandeliers, etc. Candle holders were made off wood, tin, iron, brass, pewter, and silver.

Coal oil lamps — Another name for kerosene which, prior to about 1860, was refined by roasting oil shale. Such a process made kerosene an expensive fuel — far too expensive for the average family. After the discovery of oil, coal oil became the primary source of fuel and made other fuel obsolete. Although the inventor of the original kerosene burner is unknown, the burner eventually evolved into a practical lamp, requiring little or no improvement for many years.

Crusies — The forerunner of the betty lamp, usually pear shaped and open-topped with a long wick channel and a half bail for hanging. They were messy since excess oil usually dripped out onto any surface below. The double crusie consisted of two similarly pear-shaped vessels, the upper for burning and the lower to catch the drippings. The upper pan could be tilted forward for more total use of fuel. The double crusie was also called the phoebe lamp.

Drop burner — In early glass lamps the vertical wick support tube was mounted in a plate which rested on the lip of the font, and the wick was dropped into the font. In some instances the tube was run through a cork. Later lamps had screw tops.

Float lamps — A wick supported by a cork was floated in a glass container of oil. Some lamps of this kind were hung from the ceiling while others were designed to sit on a table. Such lamps are among the earliest known.

Font — That part of the lighting device that holds the fuel supply.

Grease lamps — The general term for any lamp that burns grease.

Grisettes — Long oval iron pans used to melt fat in which rushes were soaked.

Kerosene lamps — Also known as coal oil lamps, using kerosene for fuel.

Lace makers lamps — Consisted of blown glass globes with bases for table use or with necks allowing for suspension from rope or thongs on frames of various designs. The globes were filled with water. The light from a candle or other lighting device placed near the globe or globes would magnify the light passing through them, affording improved levels of light to work by.

Lard oil lamps — Any lamp designed to burn lard oil. Since lard was the nearest to fluid of any fuel, burners were designed to convert it to liquid. Also see Argand burner, Southworth patent, and ribbon burner.

Miles patent — A milestone in lamp development. Patented in 1787, Miles was the first to construct a tight cap on the font, thereby eliminating fuel spilling.

Naphtha — A highly volatile liquid sometimes used in burning fluid lamps.

Pan lamps — The oldest type of lamp known. Any type of shallow container used to burn tallow, grease, or oil.

Patent lamps — A general term applied to all lamps with patented features.

Peg lamp — Any lamp that has a peg-shaped base, allowing it to be placed in a candle holder. In this way candle holders could be converted to bases for other types of lighting devices.

Petticoat lamp — Usually a whale oil lamp consisting of a peg lamp set in a base and resembling a woman with a narrow waist wearing a blouse and full skirt.

Phoebe lamp — Another name for a double crusie lamp.

Ribbon burner — A burner used for lard oil lamps made up of a thin copper wick support attached to the font cap and extending deep into the font. Heat from the flame would travel down the copper wick support into the font to melt the lard.

Rush light or candle — Early lights made from members of the marsh rush family. Harvested in late summer while still green, most of the outer green vortex was peeled away, leaving only a thin fibrous coating around the inner pith. After drying, the rush was soaked in tallow and then dried again. It was burned by positioning it in a holder at about 45 degrees above horizontal.

Rush light holder — A pincher device, usually of cast iron, used to hold a rush candle or rush light.

Sconce — A wall-mounted holder usually with a reflector, used primarily for candles but sometimes for other types of lighting devices.

Snuffers — One of a variety of scissorlike devices used to cut off and hold the carbonized ends of candle wicks. Snuffers were essential with early candles since the twisted wick seldom fell off of its own accord. Failure to snuff a candle would appreciably lower the level of light.

Southworth patent — A lard oil burner patented in 1842. Consisted basically of two narrow parallel copper wick supports separated by a copper plate which extended deep into the font. The copper conducted the heat of the flame and transmitted it into the font to melt the lard.

Spermaceti — A waxy substance separated from the oil of the sperm whale and used in making candles.

Stearine — A derivative of animal fats used in making quality candles.

Wick channel lamp — Another name for a crusie.

Wick support lamp — Another name for a betty lamp or other types of lamps having a half bail wick support.

Wick tube lamp — A general term for all types of lighting devices which used a tube to support the wick.

Illustration Index